GREEN CHEEKED CONURE GUIDE

Step by Step to Conure Raising, Health care, Training, Breeding, Interaction, Diet & Lot more

BRANDY ROSS

COPYRIGHT © 2023 by Steven Ross

TABLE OF CONTENTS

CHAPTER 1;
INTRODUCTION

Green-cheeked conures, which are well known for being friendly and lively creatures, are a common option for companion birds. These little parrots are native to South America and are often being sold in the market as pets. They make wonderful pets since they are smart, gregarious, and endowed with a delightful personality.

We will delve into the world of green-cheeked conures in this book and give you a thorough overview of caring/owning for them as pets. Everything you need to know about these birds will be well covered, including their appearance, behavior, environment and living conditions, food, diet and nutritional needs, health and maintenance, and reproduction/ breeding.

This book is for you if you are thinking of obtaining a green-cheeked conure as a pet whether you are a seasoned avian enthusiast or a first-time bird owner [beginners], our mission is to provide you with the proper knowledge you need to build a happy and safe environment for your feathered companion.

Along with crucial subjects like communication and behavior modification, we will talk about common health problems this birds experience and how to avoid them. You will have a solid grasp of how to care for a green-cheeked conure by the details of this book, as well as how to form a close relationship with your new pet bird

Let us explore the lovely world of green-cheeked conures bird now while you sit back and unwind.

OVERVIEW

Small green-cheeked conures bird are beloved as pets because of their friendly and amusing dispositions. They originate from South America, where they are well known for their vibrant green color, blue, yellow, and red hues in their feathers.

For those who are prepared to invest the time and effort necessary to properly care for them, green-cheeked conures will make wonderful pets. To flourish in captivity, they need a roomy cage with comfort, a healthy food/diet, frequent socializing, and training. Because they can live up to 25[twenty-five] years with appropriate care, green-cheeked conures are a long-term commitment for any prospective owner.

Reasons to consider them as pets

Listed below are some benefits of keeping green-cheeked conures as pets.

1. Playful and affectionate:

Green-cheeked conures are renowned for their affable (friendly) nature. They are excellent companion pets since they like and enjoy playing, cuddling, and interacting with their owners.

2. Low-maintenance:

Green-cheeked conures are comparatively low-maintenance pets when compared to other bigger parrots. They are a fantastic alternative or option for those with have limited time or space since they do not need as much room or care as some other parrot species as pets.

3. Appearance

Green-cheeked conures have stunning plumage that is quite vibrant and contains hues of green, blue, yellow, and red. They are gorgeous birds that can enhance any house beautifully with this appearance.

4. Intelligence

Intelligent: Green-cheeked conures birds are very clever birds who are able to replicate sounds from their background and learn tricks. Toys and puzzles may help keep these birds happy and healthy since they like cerebral stimulation practices.

5. Long lifespan

Green-cheeked conures birds can live up to 25[twenty-five] years if given the correct care

6. Social

Green-cheeked conures are very sociable creatures that take a lot of pleasure in being around people and other birds as they like social contact and are able to form close relationships with their human kin/owners.

In general, green-cheeked conures birds make wonderful pets for anyone who have the time and energy to devote to their pet bird upkeep.

CHAPTER 2: PHYSICAL CHARACTERISTICS

APPEARANCE

The look of green-cheeked conures bird is distinctive, fascinating and colorful. They are little parrots with mostly green feathers on their backs and wings and a deeper shade of green on their tails area. Their faces are colorfully marked, including a reddish-brown type patch on their foreheads and a recognizable white ring around their eyes area. Their bellies are often seen yellow or a lighter shade of green color. They can easily hold onto trees and perch because to their slender, curved beaks and feet style, which have two toes pointing forward and two pointing backward.

WEIGHT AND SIZE

Small parrots, green-cheeked conures are around 10(ten) inches (that is 25 cm) long from their beak to the end of the tail. Males are somewhat seen bigger than females, and their weight ranges from 60-80 grams on average weight. Despite their little size, they are lively, vivacious birds who need plenty of room in their housing to roam about and play. To maintain their physical and mental wellbeing of this bird, it is crucial to provide them a roomy cage, equipment and chances for play and exercise.

LIFESPAN

Green-cheeked conures survive up to 25[twenty-five] years in captivity with the right care and nourishment given.

However, a number of variables like as heredity trait, dietary habits, physical activity levels, and availability to proper veterinary care, can solely affect how long they live. To guarantee that your green-cheeked conure bird has a long and healthy life, provide them a variety of balanced food, a roomy cage, and lots of socializing, mental stimulation, and frequent veterinarian checkups.

CHAPTER 3. BEHAVIOR AND PERSONALITY

Conures with green cheeks are renowned for having a friendly and lively attitude. They are very sociable birds that take much pleasure in mingling with their humans and other close animals.

They often exhibit the following actions and personality traits:

Green-cheeked conures are energetic and active birds that like playing with toys, crossword puzzles, and other play like activities. They also like exploring their environment, enjoying climbing, and swinging.

Green-cheeked conures are loving creatures who savor time spent with their owners and snuggling. They may get devoted to their human relatives and are known to build close ties with them.

Green-cheeked conures are talkative birds meaning they take quite a lot of pleasure in interacting with both humans and other birds. With the right instruction given, they may pick up on mimicking words and sounds.

Intelligent: To maintain their happiness and general health, green-cheeked conures need cerebral activity. Activities like figuring out riddles and picking up new skills.

COMMUNICATION

Green-cheeked conures are sociable birds that interact well with their owners and other birds using a range of noises and body languages. The following are some typical means of communication green-cheeked conures exhibit:

The vocalizations of green-cheeked conures birds vary from quiet chirp's noises, coos to loud squawks, and yells. They use a variety of noises to convey their feelings, such as joy, excitement, fear, and rage, etc.

As said, they also communicate via body language. Body languages like trying to look bigger and more authoritative, puff their feathers up; alternatively, they tuck their heads in to convey submission and alter the way their bodies move to reflect certain moods.

Mimicry: Green-cheeked conures birds can be taught how to imitate human speech heard frequently and other noises with the right training.

Green-cheeked conures also communicate by making eye contact. Using direct eye contact to express their love or assert control, while it can be avoided when someone feels fearful or apprehensive to them.

In general, green-cheeked conures bird are gregarious birds that use a range of communication techniques with their owners (stay aware of its various noises and body language, as this will help you provide it the necessary socialization for it to grow).

CHAPTER 4: HOUSING AND ENVIRONMENT

Appropriate home and setting:

- Size of the cage:

The cage should be as big as it can be, at least 23 inches long, 19 inches wide, and 23-24 inches tall. As using this, measurements will give your conure adequate room to maneuver and spread its wings in their cage.

- Perches:

To encourage your conure to exercise often and to avoid foot issues arising, the cage should feature at least two [2] perches of various diameters. Provide your bird a more comfortable hold perch; real wood perches are preferred over those made of plastic or metal.

- Toys

Give them a range of toys to keep them occupied and amused in their cage. The best toys offered are those made of organic materials like wood and rope (avoid metal).

- Heat and humidity

Keep their cage in a warm, draft-free location that is between 68~78 degrees Fahrenheit.

- Lightening

Conures need 10-12 hours of daylight each day, so place their cage in a well-lit location throughout the day and make sure to keep their cage away from windows and bright sunshine to prevent overheating or drafts.

- Cleanliness

To preserve their hygiene and stop the spread of any illness, frequently clean your conure's cage and accessories in the cage. While cleaning avoid using strong chemicals or sprays to clean and instead use a disinfectant suitable for your birds.

CHAPTER 5: DIET AND NUTRITION

Green-cheeked conures need a variety of balanced diet to be healthy. Here is a diet and nutrition plan you can follow for them:

❖ Pellets:

The majority of your green-cheeked conure's feed/diet should consist of major pellets. Pick tiny parrot-specific pellets of the highest caliber made especially for parrots.

List of feed-able pellets

- Natural ZuPreem Pellets
- Daily Maintenance Pellets for Roudybush
- High-potency fine pellets from Harrison's
- Nutri-Berries by Lafeber

- Exact Rainbow Daily Diet by Kaytee Pellets
- Pellets for little parrots from Pretty Bird Daily Select
- Pellets of TOPs Organic Parrot Food
- Bonanza Hartz Bird food pellets
- Pellets of Higgins Sunburst Gourmet Blend Parrot Food
- Pellets for super parrotlet diet from Volkmann Avian Science.

❖ Fresh produce

A variety of fresh fruits and vegetables are favorite's meals of green-cheeked conures. Provide a variety of choices when it comes to fruit, such as carrots, broccoli, oranges, bananas, berries, apples, and sweet potatoes. Make careful to take out any seeds, pits, or skins from your fruits that your bird shouldn't consume.

List of allowable fruits and vegetables

- Apples
- Bananas
- Strawberries, blueberries, raspberries, and other berries
- Grapes
- Mangoes
- Pineapples
- Oranges
- Pomegranates
- Carrots
- Broccoli
- Cauliflower
- The sweet potato
- Peppers (such as bell peppers and chili peppers)
- Spinach
- Kale
- Cucumber
- Zucchini
- Butternuts, acorns, and other squash

- the beans
- Peas

❖ Nuts and seeds

Nuts and seeds should only be consumed by your bird in small amounts (25% of their diet) as treats due to their high fat content in it. Pick unsalted varieties of nuts and seeds such almonds, walnuts, pumpkin seeds, and sunflower seeds to them. Avocado fruit should not be given to birds at all since it is poisonous.

Seeds and nuts listed:

- Pumpkin seeds and sunflower seeds are both unsalted.
- (Unsalted) sesame seeds
- Flax seeds (without salt)
- Hemp seeds (without salt)
- Chia seeds (without salt)

- Almonds (without salt)
- Walnuts (without salt)
- Pistachios (without salt)
- Pecans (without salt)

❖ Water

Every day, give your green-cheeked conure bird access to ready clean, fresh water. To stop the development of germs or illness, change the water every day and clean the water dish regularly.

❖ Nutrients

In order to maintain their general health, your green-cheeked conure will need extra nutrients in their diet. To ascertain if your bird might need any extra vitamins or minerals, speak with a veterinarian or avian expert.

List of possible supplements:

- D3 vitamin
- Calcium
- fatty acids omega-3
- Probiotics
- metabolic enzymes
- Multi-vitamins
- Electrolytes

Keep in mind that not every supplement should be required for your green-chinned conure, and certain nutrients may be dangerous if given in excess to your pet. Before feeding your bird any vitamins added, always get advice from a doctor or avian expert before giving which they can assist you well in determining if your bird needs any extra vitamins or minerals to their diet and can suggest the right supplements and quantities depending on each bird's particular health requirements.

FEEDING

RECOMMENDATIONS

Offer their food/meal twice a day, both in the morning and the evening, to replicate their normal eating times. By doing this, you may keep your bird's hunger in check and prevent overeating habit.

- Provide variety

To keep your green-cheeked conure interested in their diet, provide a variety of meals to them. From time to time change up the fruits and vegetables you provide to them, as well as the pellets and treats you use.

Foods to avoid giving them include chocolate, coffee, alcohol, and anything with a high salt amount or sugar content for green-cheeked conures as these foods have the potential to damage or even kill birds.

CHAPTER 6: HEALTH AND CARE

COMMON HEALTH ISSUES

Although green-cheeked conures typically have good health (low risk of illness), like any animals, they may have problems with it. The most typical medical conditions that affect green-cheeked conures birds are vitamin deficiency, feather plucking habit, and respiratory infections. The following list of typical ailments and their remedies applies to green-cheeked conures:

Respiratory illnesses

Respiratory infections in green-cheeked conures are very common and can be brought/gotten on by bacteria, viruses, or fungus. Sneezing, coughing, nasal discharge, and breathing problems are symptoms of this illness. Your veterinarian could suggest antibiotics tab, antifungal drugs, or nebulization treatment to treat their respiratory infections. Make sure your bird's surroundings is clean and free of any dust like and other irritants to avoid respiratory diseases.

Plucking feathers

Green-cheeked conures may start plucking their own feathers because of boredom, stress, or physical discomfort. Before therapy can start, it is essential to determine the underlying reason/effect of feather plucking. The use of toys and other forms of their environmental enrichment, the treatment of underlying medical conditions, or the use of anxiety-relieving medications are all possible forms of treatment to this.

Deficiencies in vitamins

Vitamin shortages occur in green-cheeked conures as a well-known major deficiency, particularly if they are not given a well-balanced diet.

One of the most typical causes of vitamin A insufficiency is respiratory infections, skin/feather troubles, and eye difficulties. Make sure your bird has and is given a balanced diet that includes fresh fruits and vegetables to avoid any vitamin deficits. If your bird is not receiving enough nutrients from its food, your veterinarian could also suggest adding a vitamin supplement.

Signs of disease

Common green-cheeked conure sickness symptoms include:

Alterations in conduct

When unwell, a green-cheeked conure may exhibit sluggishness in behavior or listlessness. Additionally, they can show/act angrier or more aggressively than normal.

Alterations in thirst or appetite

If your green-cheeked conure is not eating or drinking as much as normal, that is a major sign of illness/disease among them.

Alterations in droppings

Bird droppings from a healthy conure bird should be solid and well formed. Droppings from your bird that start to seem watery or have a different hue might be a sign of trouble in their health.

Respiratory difficulties

Green-cheeked conures may exhibit any of the following symptoms of respiratory issues: sneezing, coughing, wheezing, or difficulty breathing.

Alterations in feather behavior or appearance

Excessive preening or scratching may be symptoms of disease, as can feather plucking or changes in feather appearance is a health disaster sign.

Nose or eye discharge

Discharge from their nose or eyes may indicate a respiratory infection or other medical conditions.

Lumpiness or swelling

A veterinarian should check for any lumps, bumps, or swelling on your green-cheeked conure bodies or below their feathers.

Advice; get veterinarian assistance as soon as you can if your green-cheeked conure exhibits any of these symptoms mentioned.

ROUTINE EXAMINATIONS AND GROOMING

For your green-cheeked conure bird to remain healthy and happy, regular exams in body and frequent grooming are crucial.

Here are some pointers on how to give your green conure bird frequent checkups and grooming:

Regular Examinations

Even though your green-cheeked conure seems healthy, essentially get them checked up by a vet at least once or twice a year. The veterinarian will do a physical examination on their body during these checkups and can advise bloodwork or other medical testing to look for any underlying health concerns in them. Regular examinations will assist in identifying health problems early, which can enhance your bird's prognosis.

Trim their nails

The sharp talons of green-cheeked conures have the potential to scratch you or harm your/their possessions. Routinely clip your bird's nails in order to avoid this and trim the tips of the nails regularly, you may use a set of specialist bird nail clippers for this.

Just be cautious not to cut the quick (the blood artery within the birds nail). You may have a veterinarian or bird groomer clip your bird's nails for you if you do not feel comfortable doing this practice.

Trimming the beak

Green-cheeked conures can have beak over growth or malformations that make it so challenging for them to feed or groom themselves. It is better to have a veterinarian or skilled bird groomer clip your bird's beak if it requires it. Beak trimming should only be carried out when absolutely shown or essential since, if done incorrectly; it may hurt or wound your bird.

Feather cutting

Trimming your green-cheeked conure's feathers might help keep them from escaping or hurting themselves in flight. Only a qualified bird groomer or veterinarian should clip feathers, nails or beaks since it may be harmful if done incorrectly.

Bathing

Giving green-cheeked conures frequent bathing will maintain their feathers all clean and healthy since they like taking proper baths. By spraying your bird with a spray bottle or putting a small bowl of water in its cage, you can offer/give it a bath. Make sure the water in there is the proper temperature and that your bird has sufficient grip on the perches to prevent any falls.

In conclusion, regular checkups and grooming can really help maintain the health and body of your green-cheeked conure.

CHAPTER 7: TRAINING AND BEHAVIOR MODIFICATION

These gregarious and clever birds can be taught to perform a wide range of behaviors and tricks. The most effective training and behavior modification techniques for green-cheeked conures will be covered in this section of this book.

Positive Discipline Training

Positive reinforcement training is the most effective method for teaching a green-cheeked conure or any other bird. This strategy/practice includes praising or rewarding positive conduct while disregarding undesirable behavior with treats. Positive reinforcement training requires a clicker, incentives, and a lot of patience to begin with.

Get your bird used to the clicker to start and give your bird an instant reward after pressing the clicker. Continue doing this process until your bird starts to connect the click with a reward.

Target Instruction

A fantastic approach to encourage your green-cheeked conure bird to come to you or go to a certain spot is via target training them. Hold a stick or their perch in front of your bird and click the clicker when they contact it with their beak to start target training them. Give your pet bird a treat right away and once your bird consistently reaches the target, repeat this technique a few other times.

Use this process on your bird to teach certain behaviors after it is used to the target. The target may be used, for instance, to train your bird to climb up onto your palm or into its cage.

Vocal Instruction

The chatty and talkative green-cheeked conures can be trained to imitate a wide range of words, sound and noises. Start by repeatedly saying a short word or phrase to your bird that you want to teach while it is listening to learn how to communicate. Make careful you speak clearly and consistently to them.

Your bird will eventually begin to connect the term with the sound of your voice that you give them. As soon as your bird has become used to the word, you can start the use of positive reinforcement training to get them to repeat it once done.

MODIFICATION OF BEHAVIOR

Birds may have their undesirable behavior that you would want changed through a process called behavior modification. It is critical to deal with any problematic behaviors your green-cheeked conure displays as soon as possible/noticed, such as biting or yelling irrelevantly.

Finding the cause for the behavior should be the first step in your bird behavior modification. For instance, your bird can be biting out of fear or rage. Once you have determined the cause of the bad behavior, you can start to change it by employing positive reinforcement training to promote alternate behavior.

Educate your bird to step up onto your hand rather than bite them, for instance, if they are biting because they are afraid of you or anything else, give your bird a reward and click the clicker each time it climbs or comes onto your hand. Your bird will eventually come to associate climbing up onto your palm with pleasant behavior after each time of practice, which will make them less inclined to bite.

Teach your bird conure a variety of tricks and behaviors while also correcting any undesirable habits that you do not work with through persistence, positive reinforcement training, and patience.

CHAPTER 8: BREEDING AND REPRODUCTION

NEEDS FOR BREEDING

To preserve the health and welfare of the birds and their progeny, breeding green-cheeked conures takes close considerable planning and preparation. The following are some essential conditions for productive green-cheeked conure breeding:

1. Age and health:

Conures must be at least 2[two] years old and in excellent health before they are permitted to reproduce or practice. They will be physically and all mature to be able to have healthy new birds because of this.

2. Diet:

For the breeding pair's and their offspring's health, giving a balanced diet is crucial. High-quality pellets, fresh clean produce, and a moderate quantity of seeds should make up the diet.

3. Nesting Box:

The breeding couple should have easy access to a nesting box where they can safe deposit their eggs. The nest box should be built of sturdy, with non-toxic materials and big enough for the couple to walk about freely in.

4. Temperature:

Green-cheeked conures are native to South America and must reproduce effectively in a warm, tropical habitat/space. A relative humidity of 50~60% and a temperature range of

74–85°F should be maintained in the breeding conure region.

5. Lighting:

Breeding requires a 12-hour light cycle of light followed by a 12-hour period of darkness to replicate a day. This mimics the cycle of natural light that initiates breeding in the wild.

Green-cheeked conures should be coupled up together before the mating season comes since they are monogamous creatures. To make sure they get along, the two(2) should be introduced gradually and constantly watched from time to time.

The female conure will deposit three-six eggs out, which she will then incubate for around 22 days after laying. She will stay in the nesting box made throughout this period and be fed by the male to make sure the eggs are growing normally, they should be checked often.

6. Hand-Feeding:

For the first few weeks of their life, the bird-chicks must be hand-fed a specific formula every two-three hours after they hatch from the eggs. This takes a lot of time and effort, as well as expert understanding/ guide on new birds of the chick's dietary requirements.

7. Weaning:

The chicks may be weaned and progressively introduced to solid diets after around 8[eight] weeks. During this period of time, it is important to keep a careful/close eye on them to make sure they are receiving enough balanced food and growing normally.

It takes meticulous proper planning, preparation, and in-depth familiarity with these pet birds' food and environmental requirements to successfully breed or mate them.

MAKING NESTS AND DEPOSITING EGGS

These birds have certain distinctive traits and habits that are crucial to comprehend and understand when it comes to nesting and egg laying.

Age and Mating Behavior:

Green-cheeked conures reach their sexual maturity between the ages of one~two. They are lifelong bird partners because they are monogamous birds, and they often engage in courting rituals/behaviors including eating, grooming themselves, and vocalizing.

Green-cheeked conures normally breed in the wild between the months of October and around April. They will start looking for a good nesting location at this time. In captivity or owned as pets, they often accept a nest box or an appropriate hollow branch or wood.

Egg Laying:

The female green-cheeked bird conure will begin to deposit the eggs laid after a nesting location has been found or determined. There may be anywhere between 2(two) and 6(six) eggs deposited, with an average clutch size of 4(four). Ordinarily, eggs are then deposited every other day until the clutch process is finished.

The male and female green-cheeked conures in the breeding process will alternate turning over the eggs during incubation. The parents alternately perch on the laid eggs to keep them warm and guarantee healthy growth throughout the 23~26 day of their incubation period.

Development of the Chick and Hatching:

Once the green cheeked eggs hatch, the chicks are entirely reliant/dependent on their parents for nourishment and proper care. The chicks will spend around 6-8 weeks in the nest, growing quickly and beginning to slowly get feathers. The parents will continue to feed and tend to them throughout this care period, often regurgitating food to do so.

Fledging and Independence:

The chicks will start to explore outside of the nest after they have grown all of their feathers and have acquired their flying muscles. They will be fed and cared for by the parents until they are completely independent, which typically happens 10 to 12 weeks after hatching.

TAKING CARE OF CHICKS

Taking care of young green-cheeked conure birds chicks

Keep the Chicks Warm:

Green-cheeked conure chicks should always be kept all warm, particularly in the early stages of the chick development. For the first week, the brooder temperature should be adjusted/kept at around 95~100°F (35–

37.8°C), then it should be progressively dropped over the next several weeks to about 84°F (29.4°C). To keep the bird chicks warm, use a heating pad or heat light in their house.

Ensure Adequate Nutrition:

In order for green-cheeked conure chicks to develop healthily, their food must be well-balanced and nutrient-rich for them. You should give them a premium hand-feeding formula made especially for parrots that is readily accessible in the local marketplace. Every two-three hours, feed the bird chicks the formula that has been prepared in accordance with the manufacturer's instructions in the feed.

Cleaning:

Maintaining a clean and sanitary environment is very essential for the survival of green-cheeked conure new born chicks. Each time a feeding process occurs, carefully clean the brooder and any feeding apparatus used. To avoid the development of dangerous germs, illness or parasites, replace any filthy bedding or nesting materials consistently.

The right socialization and engagement of green-cheeked conure chicks with people and other birds is essential for their vocal development. Spend time with them each day, conversing words and sounds with them and being kind with them, as this will enable them to form close relationships with people/owmers and grow into well-behaved pets.

Follow up on their health:

Keep an eye on the green-cheeked conure chicks' growth and health on a regular basis. Keep an eye out for any symptoms of disease, such as vomiting, diarrhea, or loss of appetite, and seek veterinarian treatment if required as seen. To track their growth development, keep a record of their weight, food regimen, and change in behavior.

Care for green-cheeked conure chicks needs perseverance, close pet commitment, and meticulousness. You can assist in ensuring that they develop into healthy and happy adult conure birds by giving them a warm and sanitary habitat, well nourishing food, interaction opportunities, and frequent health checks.

A GUIDE TO BREEDING

An instruction manual for breeding two mature green-cheeked conures is provided below:

- *Choosing your breeding couple is the first step.*

Choosing a suitable breeding healthy pair of green-cheeked conures is the first stage to breeding. Ensure that both birds are well fit for breeding, active, and fully healthy. As younger birds could not be mature enough to procreate new borns, choose birds that are at least 2(two) years old. To prevent inbreeding, it is ideal to choose a male and female green cheeked who are unrelated to one another.

- *Step 2: Creating a conducive environment for reproduction*

After choosing your better breeding partner, you must set up a conducive breeding environment for both of them. A big breeding cage that is at least 23 inches wide, 24 inches deep, and 29-30 inches tall is the best setting for green-cheeked conures to breed in. A nest box, perches, and a ton of toys and enrichment items should all be included in their breeding cage.

- *Step 3: Nutrition and Diet*

It is critical to provide your breeding pair a very nutritious, well-balanced diet. Offer a diet that includes premium parrot pellets, seasonal produce, bird cereals, and fresh fruits with vegetables to ensure that your birds' bones are strong and well healthy, you should also give them a calcium rich supplement.

- *Introduce the breeding pair in step four.*

Gradually slowly introduce the breeding couple to one another, beginning with short meeting intervals of watched interaction. You keep both of them in the breeding cage together if they get along well.

- *Monitoring breeding behavior is step five.*

Your birds will start to display breeding behavior with each other after they have formed a relationship and feel at ease in their new home. This include time spent in the nest box, preening, and regurgitating food to one another(male and female). Make sure to keep a careful eye on their activity to make sure they are successfully mating and getting ready to deposit laid eggs.

- *Providing a nest box is step six.*

Green-cheeked conures like building their nests in dim, confined areas. Set up a bird nest box with dimensions of at least 12(twelve) inches on each side, 12 inches on the bottom, and 17 inches on top. Clean, soft nesting materials like shredded paper or untreated wood shavings should be used to line the nest box.

- *Step 7: Laying eggs and incubating them*

Each clutch of green-cheeked conures normally contains 4~6 eggs. After laying eggs for 23-28 days, they will start to hatch. Crucial to provide your birds lots of quality food and water during this period, as well as to maintain the nest box tidy and pest-free space.

- *Eighth step: rearing the chicks*

The chicks will be reliant on their parents for food and care after they have hatched out. The breeding couple will require a lot of food and water since they will need to also feed the chicks regularly from there meals. Add hand-feeding formula to their diet as a supplement then after 6 to 8 weeks, the chicks will fledge and be able to be removed from their parents.

- *Step 9: Care after breeding*

Giving your birds a vacation and allowing them to recuperate well after the breeding season is crucial. Additionally, now is a good time to cleanse the nest box and breeding cage and to provide your pet birds new toys and enrichment supplies/formulas.

Breeding green-cheeked conures parrots involves persistence, strong commitment, and meticulousness, but with the right preparation and consideration, it can be a satisfying experience and easy practice.

CHAPTER 9: FINAL/PERSONAL RECOMMENDATIONS FOR KEEPING A GREEN-CHEEKED CONURE AS A PET.

o Give your green-cheeked conure a roomy, exciting environment/home with plenty of toys, perches, and chances for exercise.

o Their health and wellbeing depend on a healthy and varied parrot diet that includes quality premium pellets, fresh fruits, vegetables, and grains.

o Their mental and emotional wellbeing depend on regular engagement and socializing practice with their owner.

o Green-cheeked conures parrots require a lot of relaxation and quiet time, but they also like playing and receiving attention from their owners.

o It is very crucial to get regular veterinarian checkups to keep a close eye on their health and stave against any infections.

o Keep their surroundings tidy, neat, up to date, providing them with new food, and water each day, as well as a clean illness free cage.

o Being very gregarious creatures in nature, green-cheeked conures parrots enjoy interacting with other birds. If you can, consider acquiring them a friend or setting up playdates with other birds.

THE END

THANK YOU AND GOODLUCK

Made in the USA
Columbia, SC
04 November 2024

45649824R00037